Funny Bone Jokes

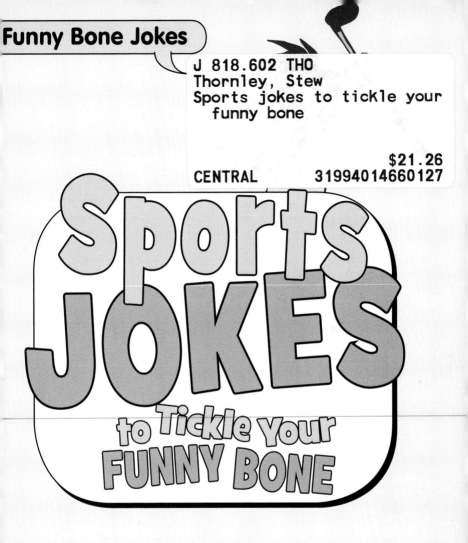

Sports JOKES to Tickle Your FUNNY BONE

Stew Thornley

Enslow Elementary

an imprint of

Enslow Publishers, Inc.

40 Industrial Road
Box 398
Berkeley Heights, NJ 07922
USA

http://www.enslow.com

Enslow Elementary, an imprint of Enslow Publishers, Inc.

Enslow Elementary® is a registered trademark of Enslow Publishers, Inc.

Copyright © 2011 by Stew Thornley.

Library of Congress Cataloging-in-Publication Data

Thornley, Stew.
    Sports jokes to tickle your funny bone / Stew Thornley.
        p. cm. — (Funny bone jokes)
    Includes bibliographical references and index.
    Summary: "Includes jokes, limericks, knock-knock jokes, tongue twisters, and fun facts about baseball, basketball, football, hockey, golf, and more, and describes how to write your own jokes"—Provided by publisher.
    ISBN 978-0-7660-3545-4
    1. Sports—Juvenile humor. I. Title.
    PN6231.S65T46 2010
    818'.602—dc22

                2010006170

Printed in the United States of America

122010 Lake Book Manufacturing, Inc., Melrose Park, IL

10 9 8 7 6 5 4 3 2 1

Illustration Credits: © Clipart.com, a division of Getty Images, all clipart.

Cover Illustration: © Clipart.com, a division of Getty Images.

Contents

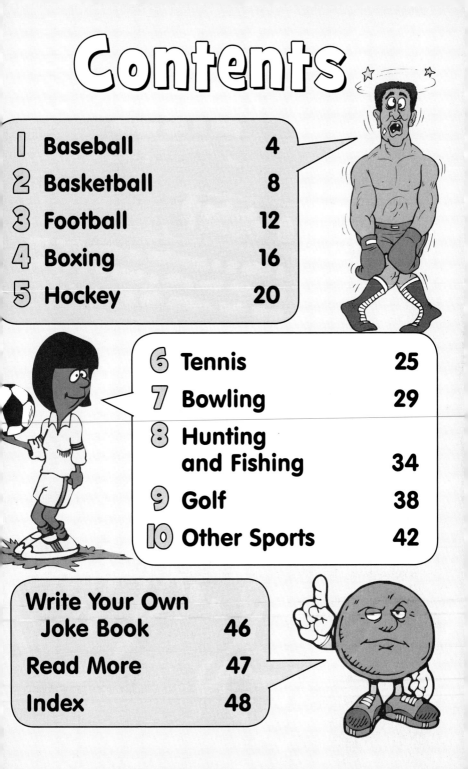

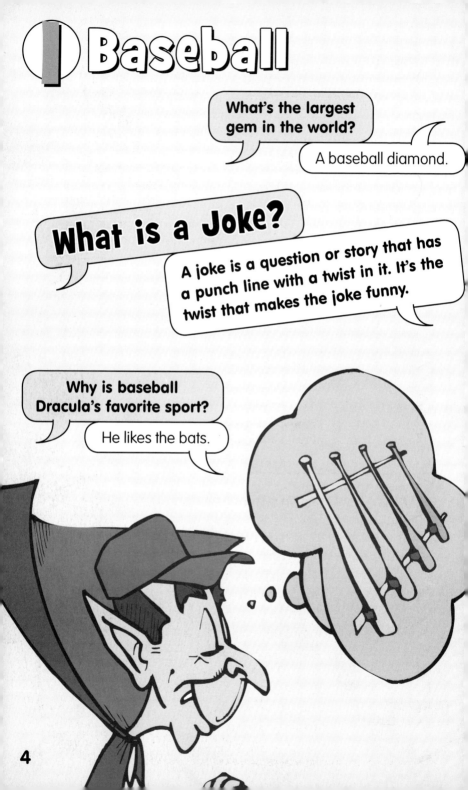

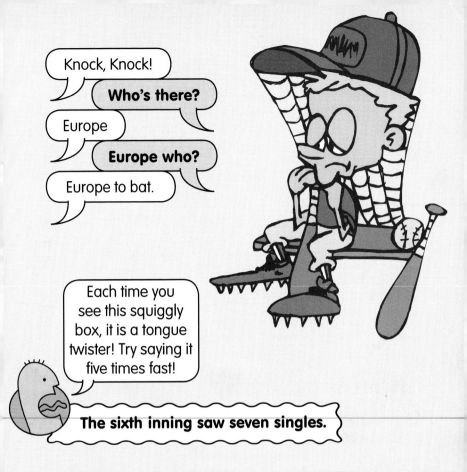

Knock, Knock!

Who's there?

Europe

Europe who?

Europe to bat.

Each time you see this squiggly box, it is a tongue twister! Try saying it five times fast!

The sixth inning saw seven singles.

FUN FACTS

IT'S TRUE.

You may have heard the name Abner Doubleday if you are a baseball fan. Many people think he invented baseball in Cooperstown, New York. This isn't true. The game goes back to before Abner Doubleday was even born. It is a form of other bat-and-ball games that had been played in England for a long time. Even though baseball wasn't invented in Cooperstown, New York, that small village is now the home of the Baseball Hall of Fame.

Knock, Knock!

Who's there?

Uriah.

Uriah who?

Keep Uriah the ball.

Where do you keep your mitt when you're in the car?

The glove compartment.

Betty's a better batter.

Why does it take longer to go from second to third base than from first to second base?

Because there is a shortstop between second and third.

FUN FACTS

Babe Ruth was one of the greatest baseball players ever. He played in the major leagues from 1914 to 1935. Most of the seasons were with the New York Yankees. He changed the game with his slugging. Before Ruth came along, home runs were not common. Ruth was the first player to hit at least 30 home runs in a season in the majors. His biggest total was 60 home runs in 1927.

IT'S TRUE.

The field Lucinda loved to roam.
She covered turf from Natchez to Nome.
And with her strong arm
she did baserunners harm,
as she often threw them out at home.

② Basketball

What is an incredible story about a basketball center called?

A tall tale.

Jump shot, set shot. Jump shot, set shot. Jump shot, set shot.

What team did the prince want to be on?

The Sacramento Kings.

Knock, Knock!

Who's there?

Safari.

Safari who?

Safari are winning the game.

The player was known as a punk.
Opponents said his game was junk.
He stopped their trash talk
when he flew like a hawk
and came down with a thunderous dunk.

WOOSH!

Knock, Knock!

Who's there?

Sara.

Sara who?

Sara player
I can count on to
make a basket?

What is a Limerick?

Limericks are five-line poems. The end of the first, second, and fifth lines of the verse rhyme. The third and fourth lines, which are shorter, also rhyme.

9

FUN FACTS

Dr. James Naismith is credited with inventing the game of basketball in 1891. He was an instructor at a YMCA International Training School in Springfield, Massachusetts. He wanted something his students could do inside during the winter, so he came up with the idea of having them throw a ball into a basket 10 feet off the floor. The first game was played December 21, 1891.

IT'S TRUE.

Deirdre's dribble drew defenders.

3 Football

Which football game do cats like to watch?

The Goldfish Bowl.

Why do football players wear helmets on their heads?

Because they don't fit on their feet.

What do centers wear on the feet?

Hiking shoes.

FUN FACTS

In the National Football League (NFL), teams play for the championship in the Super Bowl. In Canada, the championship game is called the Grey Cup. There are some differences between the games in the United States and Canada. The playing field in Canada is larger. It is 110 yards long. In the United States, the distance between the end zones in 100 yards. In the United States, teams have four tries to get a first down. They have only three tries in Canada.

IT'S TRUE.

13

Big Boomer could move like a cat.
He shook off his defender like a gno
Two others came in.
Boomer gave them a spin.
They ran into each other with a spla

Knock, Knock!

Who's there?

Halibut.

Halibut who?

Halibut you let me go in and play, Coach?

Barry barreled boldly beyond the blocking back.

What is a Tongue Twister?

Tongue twisters can be funny. When you try to say them over and over, you might slip up and say something different.

Fullback fumbles, fullback fumbles, fullback fumbles.

The Heisman Trophy goes to the top college football player every year. The only player to win the award twice was Archie Griffin of Ohio State. He won it in both 1974 and 1975. Eight Heisman Trophy winners were good enough to be voted into the Pro Football Hall of Fame. They are Roger Staubach, Paul Hornung, O. J. Simpson, Doak Walker, Barry Sanders, Earl Campbell, Marcus Allen, and Tony Dorsett.

IT'S TRUE.

A quarterback was looking fine
until his team neared the goal line.
He started to shake.
The play he could not make.
It was said that he had quit tryin'.

What do receivers catch after running downfield?

Their breath.

4 Boxing

What kind of a dog could punch you?

A boxer.

Knockout Nelson kneeled needlessly.

What do you call a boxer who gets beat up in a fight?

A sore loser.

Doogie McDaniel boxed for many years. When he died and was buried, his tombstone had written on it, "You can stop counting. I'm not getting up."

Perry packed a punch with power.

Did you hear about the boxing referee who used to work at a space rocket launching site?

If a fighter was knocked down he'd count ten, nine, eight, seven . . .

When the Crusher forgot to look
as Bruiser was starting to cook,
the Crusher looked right,
Bruiser connected with might,
and a left hook was all that it took.

Knock, Knock!

Who's there?

Radio.

Radio who?

Radio not, the match is about to start.

Will's wallop wowed the watchers.

Knock, Knock!

Who's there?

Ivana.

Ivana who?

Ivana land a solid punch.

The boxer danced around like a cat.
It seemed his feet didn't even touch the mat
until he let down his guard,
got hit exceedingly hard,
and was knocked to the mat quite flat.

Mel mashed Matt, who met the mat.

FUN FACTS

Muhammad Ali won the world's heavyweight boxing title three times. He won the title the first time when he beat Sonny Liston in 1964. In 1974, Ali beat George Foreman to win the championship again. Leon Spinks beat Ali in 1978. However, in a rematch later in the year, Ali beat Spinks. He was the world champion for the third time.

IT'S TRUE.

Wally won when Wendall wilted.

5 Hockey

How do hockey players kiss?

They pucker up.

How bad was the Panthers hockey team?

They were so bad that even their cheerleaders booed them.

The machine that cleans the ice between periods is called a Zamboni. It was invented by a man named Frank Zamboni in the 1940s. A Zamboni is driven around the rink. It has a blade in the back that shaves off a thin surface of the ice. It also cleans up the shavings of the ice that have been left by players skating across it. Water is sprayed to lay down a new surface of the ice.

Knock, Knock!

Who's there?

Ya.

Ya who?

Ya who, I scored a goal!

FUN FACTS

Wayne Gretzky scored more goals than any player in the history of hockey. He played for the Edmonton Oilers, Los Angeles Kings, St. Louis Blues, and New York Rangers in the National Hockey League. Gretzky scored a total of 1,487 goals in the National Hockey League. Gretzky was known as "The Great One."

IT'S TRUE.

What is the hardest foot to buy a hockey skate for?

A square foot.

Knock, Knock!

Who's there?

Justin.

Justin who?

You're Justin time for the face-off.

Face-off circle, face-off circle, face-off circle.

Red line, blue line, red line, blue line, red line, blue line.

Tennis 6

Why did Cinderella get kicked off the tennis team?

Because she ran away from the ball!

When does a tennis match get noisy?

When a player raises a racquet.

Knock, Knock!

Who's there?

Ketchup.

Ketchup who?

I need to ketchup if I'm going to win!

Dave said to his coach, "My doctor says I can't play tennis."

The coach replied to Dave, "I could have told you that."

The biggest event in tennis is played in Wimbledon, England, each year. The tournament usually starts late in June and ends on the second Sunday in July. It was first held in 1877. The Wimbledon tournament is now watched on television by an estimated one billion people around the world every year.

FUN FACTS

We won, we won, we won, we won!

Competitors carry out courtesy on the court.

A big fellow named McGee,
for success, his serve was the key.
Another one comes.
It whistles and hums.
The fans yell and scream, "Oh, Gee!"

Knock, Knock!

Who's there?

Woo.

Woo who?

Woo who,
we won!

27

FUN FACTS

Serena and Venus Williams are sisters. They are also among the top female tennis players in the world. On July 5, 2008, the Williamses played one another for the singles championship. Venus won. The sisters then teamed up for the doubles championship. They defeated Lisa Raymond and Samantha Stosur. Within a matter of hours, Venus won two Wimbledon championships.

IT'S TRUE.

Betsy Blaster had a grimace on her face
when she hit the ball at a rapid pace.
She knew it was fine.
It didn't hit the line.
Betty had served up a most-wicked ace.

Bowling 7

FUN FACTS

In 10-pin bowling, the highest score is 300. It is called a perfect game. To score 300, a bowler must throw 12 strikes. Not many people get perfect games, but a lot of bowlers get "turkeys." A turkey is three strikes in a row.

IT'S TRUE.

Knock, Knock!

Who's there?

Anita.

Anita who?

Anita strike.

Carrie's curving ball careened off course, costing her a cool score.

Bingo had a marvelous curve.
The ball, it would dip, hook, and swerve.
He didn't try to hurry
and never did worry
for Bingo had plenty of nerve.

Barry and Bitsy bowled for big bucks.

Why is a good bowler a bad baseball player?

Because he gets so many strikes.

The distance down a bowling alley is 60 feet. This is about the same distance from the pitcher's mound to home plate in baseball. The lanes are 43 inches wide. Bowling pins are 15 inches high. They are also 15 inches around at their greatest width. Bowling balls in 10-pin bowling can be as heavy as 16 pounds. Good bowlers can make their balls curve (or hook). This allows the ball to hit the pins at a better angle and makes it more likely for all the pins to fall.

IT'S TRUE.

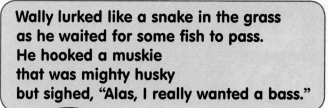

Wally lurked like a snake in the grass
as he waited for some fish to pass.
He hooked a muskie
that was mighty husky
but sighed, "Alas, I really wanted a bass."

Knock, Knock!

Who's there?

Dewey.

Dewey who?

Dewey have to keep fishing out here in the rain?

Cindy and Sandy were hiking through the woods when a huge bear jumped out in front of them.

Sandy immediately pulled off her hiking boots, reached into her knapsack, and pulled out a pair of tennis shoes.

"What are you doing?" said Cindy. "You can't outrun the bear!"

"I don't have to," said Sandy. "All I have to do is outrun you."

35

FUN FACTS

Minnesota is a state with more than 10,000 lakes. Minnesotans love to fish on those lakes. One of their favorite fish is a walleye. They are called walleyes because their eyes reflect light. This helps a walleye see and find food at night. Baudette, Minnesota, calls itself the "Walleye Capital of the World." People going to Baudette are greeted by "Willie Walleye," a huge statue of a walleye on the edge of the city.

IT'S TRUE.

Knock, Knock!

Who's there?

Wood.

Wood who?

Wood you keep quiet? You're scaring the deer away.

Willie wished for a fish
to put in his dish.

Harriet was hunting all day
hoping to find some big prey.
She was not pleased
when someone sneezed
and scared all the animals away.

Pete perched on his pad
and plucked a perch.

Golf balls are made of different materials. They may have a rubber ball inside. It could be surrounded by rubber windings. Hundreds of years ago, golf balls were made of wood. Later, they were made of feathers that were stuffed into a leather pouch. The pouch was sewn into the shape of a ball. Feather balls didn't work very well. If it rained, they would soak up water and be hard to hit very far.

IT'S TRUE.

Harry wanted to be a golf star.
He swung and hit the ball far.
But when the ball started to slice
Harry said something not nice
As he finished with a six over par.

39

EEYYAHH!

Why did Tarzan spend so much time on the golf course?

He was perfecting his swing.

FUN FACTS

Golfers use different words for their scores. Many have to do with birds. The word "par" is used for how many strokes it should take to get the ball in the hole. Golfers that can get the ball in the hole with one stroke less than par have hit a "birdie." An "eagle" is two strokes under par, and an "albatross" means three under par.

IT'S TRUE.

Knock, Knock!

Who's there?

Goat.

Goat who?

Goat to the green with your next shot?

Ann's ball was four feet from the cup.
As she putted, her friend yelled "Whassup?"
Ann waved her putter.
She started to sputter,
"When I'm hitting the ball, shuddup!"

Knock, Knock!

Who's there?

Boo.

Boo who?

Don't cry, you'll make your next putt!

Pete was the star of the track meet.
As he ran with swift-moving feet,
humans cheered,
animals leered,
the birds even started to tweet.

What kind of animal do you not want to play games with?

A cheetah.

Knock, Knock!

Who's there?

Cargo.

Cargo who?

Cargo fast enough to win the race.

Devon's coach told him to get in shape by running four miles every day. A few days later, Devon called and said, "Coach, come and pick me up. I'm 20 miles from home."

Knock, Knock!

Who's there?

Randy.

Randy who?

Randy mile in under four minutes.

Bob is a master at chess.
He plays with great finesse.
His opponents hate
to hear "Checkmate!"
It causes them too much stress.

FUN FACTS

IT'S TRUE.

One of the biggest car races is the Indianapolis 500. It is held every year around Memorial Day. The first race was held in 1911. The track in Indianapolis is two-and-a-half miles around. That means drivers have to go 200 laps to reach 500 miles. The record for the most wins is four. A. J. Foyt, Rick Mears, and Al Unser have each won the Indianapolis 500 four times.

Write Your Own Joke Book

HERE'S WHAT YOU WILL NEED:

- paper
- colored pencils, pens, or markers
- old magazines (optional)

DIRECTIONS:

1. Fold a sheet of white paper in half, and then in half in the other direction, to make the cover and inside of your joke book.

2. Remember jokes you've heard, copy your favorites from this book or other books, or create your own silly sayings, riddles, and jokes. You may want to pick a theme like sports. Use your crayons, colored markers, or pencils to write and illustrate your jokes. You can also cut out pictures from old magazines to illustrate your joke book.

3. Tickle funny bones by sharing your joke book with others.

Read More

Books

Chmielewski, Gary. *The Sports Zone: Jokes, Riddles, Tongue Twisters, and "Daffynitions."* Chicago, Ill.: Norwood House Press, 2008.

Phillips, Bob. *Awesome Knock Knock Jokes for Kids.* Eugene, Ore.: Harvest House Publishers, 2006.

Walton, Rick, and Ann Walton. *Foul Play: Sports Jokes That Won't Strike Out.* Minneapolis, Minn.: Carolrhoda Books, 2005.

Weitzman, Ilana, Eva Blank, Rosanne Green, and Alison Benjamin. *Jokelopedia: The Biggest, Best, Silliest, Dumbest Joke Book Ever.* New York: Workman Publishing Company, 2006.

Internet Addresses

Jokes for Kids
<http://www.activityvillage.co.uk/kids_jokes.htm>

NIEHS Kids' Pages: Jokes, Humor, and Trivia
<http://kids.niehs.nih.gov/jokes.htm>

Index

A
ace, 28
albatross, 40
Ali, Muhammad, 19

B
baseball, 4–7, 33
basketball, 8–11
bear, 34, 35
bowling, 29–33
boxing, 16–19

C
car racing, 42, 43, 44, 45
cheerleader, 22, 42
curve, 32, 33

D
Doubleday, Abner, 5
down, 13
dribble, 11
dunk, 9

E
end zone, 13
England, 5, 26

F
fishing, 34, 35, 36
football, 12–15

G
golf, 29, 38–41
Gretzky, Wayne, 22
Grey Cup, 13
Griffin, Archie, 15

H
Heisman Trophy, 15
hockey, 20–24
hunting, 34, 37

I
Indianapolis 500, 44
inning, 5

J
joke, 4

L
limerick, 9

N
Naismith, James, 11
National Football League (NFL), 13

National Hockey League, 22

P
par, 39, 40
pin, 29, 33

Q
quarterback, 15

R
running, 43, 44
Ruth, Babe, 7

S
soccer, 42
strike, 30, 31, 33
Super Bowl, 13

T
10-pin bowling, 31, 33
tennis, 25–28
tongue twister, 14

W
walleye, 36
Wimbledon, 26, 28

Y
Yankees, 7

Z
Zamboni, 21